Poetic Shades of Life

The Final Scripts

Mr. Bad

Order this book online at www.trafford.com
or email orders@trafford.com

Most Trafford titles are also available at major online book retailers.

Printed in the United States of America.

ISBN: 978-1-4669-8347-2 (sc)
ISBN: 978-1-4669-8349-6 (hc)
ISBN: 978-1-4669-8348-9 (e)

Library of Congress Control Number: 2013909279

Trafford rev. 09/20/2013

 www.trafford.com

North America & international
toll-free: 1 888 232 4444 (USA & Canada)
fax: 812 355 4082

Contents

Introduction

The poetry that is contained within this book is a sequence of events and is to be acknowledged in the future by those individuals, who have been involved to create this book, whether it be a fable, fiction, non fiction, a figment of my imagination, or just the plain truth. This book, which I call The Final Scripts is intended to be a final edition of poetry to my previously written books, Poetic Shades of Life 1, 2, and 3. My intention is to provide the truth, insight to things that have happened, belief in my sanity, and even embarrassment for others. My interest in poetry began, after I returned from a comfortable living style in Germany.

Upon my arrival in The United States, after my divorce and returning again, my brother granted me rights to live with him, his wife, and his children, until I could reestablish my grounds for myself. I began working at a fast food restaurant as a cook for two years, and I was attending the university at the same time and enjoying chat time on the Internet through the use of my own computer, as I did my homework always late at night. I started entering sweepstakes and lotteries through a web site called, EZSWEEPS, and thereafter, I started receiving telephone calls from Canada telling me I had a parcel with my winnings, which was at the office of the customs and that a payment needed to be made. The telephone calls then led me to trouble with my brother's telephone bill because then I was owing approximately three hundred dollars in rent and telephone bills and I got thrown into homelessness and out on the streets of Toledo.

However, after being homeless I then became a stay at a man's apartment who also worked for my same employer and I was still attending the university. I then also sensed being spied upon outside my classroom door, by what seemed to be my daughter, along with the law and I was also hearing that I won some amount of money. I then during my stay at this man's apartment, doing homework by myself, tried to have a go at my Japanese instructor, who was my teacher at the university in Japanese language classes. I sensed in the heat of this all that I was being followed and it upset me, so I had been yelling in anger because I felt harassed. The man who I was living with was to me strange in his ways about having the door open at all, but then he began to leave the door cracked open all night with the chain latched that was upon it. It seemed to me that someone was watching me all night, as I slept, and it seemed pretty creepy to me. My stay there became unpleasant, as I sensed my daughter was spying on me, after I had called her in Germany. I was then led again to homelessness and I believe this man also had enough from the dumb behavior that my daughter was playing.

My further adventure led me to falling grades, quitting school, mental stress, and living with a Spanish friend and his family, after sleeping in my vehicle in winter without any heat because of a heater core defect. So, I then took part in a Spanish household renting a room and I still sensed and heard that I was being followed and talked about. My stay there then seemed to end because of whatever reason, which then led me to homelessness and sleeping in my automobile with a defective heater core again.

Thereafter, I became a job at a local convenience mart where the owner was an Arab and at the same time I was also employed with a previous employer from the temporary service agency, without the agency. At this time I was offered from the previous employer to rent a three bedroom house by myself, which I did. At this time I was still being followed and yet by more individuals, a young blonde and her parents were pondering upon me. So, at this point, I had what seemed to be the detective's office, my daughter, the Japanese woman, and a young blonde girl behind me and the stress started to accumulate.

It then became apparent that my daughter had got herself involved with the Arab individual or owner of this convenience mart, for whom I worked and trouble began to role. I had confronted him several times with questions of knowing and willingly hiding facts about my daughter perusing me, but I was told that this was not true and maybe there was something wrong with me.

As time went on and I was working for my Landlord and this convenience mart, the Jordanian individual, I started hearing people outside my house joking around and spying upon me, as I wrote my poetry, which came to be mostly about them. They were outside my house and there were always different individuals and it seemed this Arab individual, Mo the ho, decided he was going to scare, harass, and attempt to manipulate my daughter from me, as they played their silly games outside my house, believing I was unaware of this. So then, after I was off work, which was usually after midnight, I heard that they were outside my house and they played games on my mentality and they were passing drugs to the girls, my daughter and the blonde, Sheri. As time went on with the blonde girl Sheri, who at this time had been spending time with her father and a detective outside my house, watching the others and me secretly, I became stressed out by all of this. The stress and stalking even stretched to my other employer, who was also my Landlord, so I became stressed not only in the evening but night and day.

Apparently, after all the stress and talk of me being crazy, it seemed the talk was so that they could hide the truth. I then got fired from the convenience mart, as they created a lie and said that I had broken in his store and robbed him, which was not true, but he used this excuse to play further games upon me. I then went two doors down to a service station to work for extra cash and then this owner of the service station, Mickey, began hanging outside my house with Mo the ho and was trying to be the baby-sitter for the young blonde, who was trying to become her rights to talk to me. Then I became yet another spying individual, a Hollywood movie star named, Jennifer, outside my house. From this point on there was talk of cash I had won and not just a little, but a lot and my understanding of it was that, Jennifer, claimed and payed delivery of a check and automobile I had won from Micropuff.

I had then during this time also created six songs on an organ I owned and I was also entering sweepstakes and lotteries galore on the Internet and by postal mail. I had at this time also drew up plans for an invention to be patented, I had written several poetry books with a contract on the first one, and I had all these individuals spying on me and I was beginning to be crazy. So, I had the blonde girl fighting for my rights to my cash against my daughter, who tried with help from her Arab friend to say I was crazy, I had the second Arab or Palestinian individual trying to steal my blonde girl, as the detective was watching this all, and I also had this Hollywood actress trying to get me too and break up my relationship with the blonde girl, Sheri. The stress then poured upon my blonde girlfriend and she, from what I gathered, invited another to help her against all the wrong doers, The Kid, a well known rapper, who also comes from Hollywood and was born I believe around the motor city area of Detroit.

The stalking and stress became at this point unbearable for any normal individual, which I seemed not to be but stressed and terrorized I was. From the talk I heard at this point my daughter had been abused and beat, along with scared to death by her friend, Mo the ho. The actress who at this point had claimed and paid delivery of a million dollar check and a new Ford Explorer SUV, I won from Micropuff, was not authorized to say hello, before my girlfriend, the one I grew to love, had turned eighteen, or her father authorized her the right to speak or live with me. The stress became so bad that I even had to write Marcy Kaptur's office, the congress woman in my home town, and even visit the mayor's office in my home town, and also write the president of The United States in regards to the whereabouts of my money and the stalking upon me that I had been hearing about, which to my belief was taking place.

Then, as if all was not enough already, another individual from Hollywood came into the picture, after an email from me, Eva, who I saw on a cooking show being sponsored and she was someone looking for a relationship with a man for her and her daughter. So, I did then send an email to Rachael, the sponsor, but told her Eva would be lucky, if she even passed the check-point that the government had now established, as they were watching the two male Arab individuals playing games and Jennifer acting jealous and ridiculous. At this point this book is finished and I have the mayor, the president, a congress woman, both my daughters, the detective's office, two Hollywood actresses, the young blonde, and the Kid following me, trying to figure out, as I do also, what the hell is going on.

To the reader I can only hope that the poetry is enjoyable and that they should never go through such a tragic sequence of events, as to where their live is destructed and terrorized as mine has been.

Shadow of a Woman

A lonely life and a prayer for one.
A call to God with a song.
I look to the skies and into the sun.
I wish for a thing and a thong with a ding and a dong.

From the darkest depths of the silence comes a whisper.
Out of the light of darkness appears a shadow.
A mumble becomes a rumble, as a voice becomes crisper.
Like a snake armed with its rattle.

The sun's distance brings the moon's battle.
The day's brightness brings the night's creepers.
The sound is of a sheep, but then there are cattle.
The whisper becomes to be a shout and the weepers
are then sleepers.

A line becomes to a curve with its matter.
The lightness carries a figure of a shadow.
A dream becomes reality, as I wish I had her.
The silent stream's flow brings a canoe with a paddle.

From the darkness comes a figure with the shape of a wife.
A shape of darkness with the light of the free.
Shadow of a woman and a life.
The darkness is lit and now I see.

5-1-07   Mr. Bad

This poem "Shadow of a Woman" was written because I am aware that a young blonde girl is following me. I wait for her to come to me from hiding, like out of the dark and say hello to me. I have been waiting for some time now for her with a wedding song I created and a lot of love. There have been, as I have heard, friends who attempt to convince her father that I am a nice fellow and a good man for his daughter. There is also my jealous daughter, along with a Hollywood actress, who attempts to divide us. It seems the Hollywood actress had claimed and paid for the delivery or a one million dollar check, along with a new 2006 Ford Explorer I won from Micropuff, but there seems to be some bribery involved in order for me to receive what is mine.

Behind Closed Doors

There were the places with no faces, but voices with their own choices.
Indeed there was one dumb like a bum and she drank the rum.
She stood behind closed doors squeaking like hoists'.
I had all the answers and she must have blemished like a plum.

So, she did try to be sneaky and say I was tweaky.
Her voice I did hear and I gave her fear.
It is true now that she is the freaky.
The facts are in now and they are sincere.

Behind closed doors she stood to listen.
It was all so stupid and she was a cupid.
She did not scream, but she had to listen.
Yes, it is true that cupid is stupid.

Even as I slept, she crept.
She stalked and the cracks she caulked.
She was spying and dying, as she wept.
She was behind closed doors, as she talked.

Molested and beat she was, as she tried to hide.
Like a red curtain behind closed doors she was flirting.
She did indeed play her game, but on the wrong side.
Behind closed doors she was hurting.

6-18-07   Mr. Bad

"Behind Closed Doors" is a poem I wrote about my oldest daughter secretly following me around and getting herself in trouble. It has now become clear to me, of all the troubles I have been having. A daughter had been called and was following me around while she got involved with a male, who has beat and been threatening to hurt her, if she came to me. He seems to be using her for some sort of conspiracy against me and trying to stop the sweepstake winnings I had heard of winning.

Crazy and Lazy?

I labored, sweat, starved, and craved.

I looked, listened, chased, and shouted.

They attempted to lay my path, but it was not paved.

They talked of crazy and lazy, but it was doubted.

There was the Po-Po and Toto and I heard who liked and who hated.

There were the rangers and the manger and I knew the stranger.

The game was started and the traps were laid, as I bated.

The players there were and I was the slayer, as I used love

and my anger.

Crazy and lazy, but actually only hazy!

I chocked, they joked, I smoked, they coked.

I heard the rumors of boomers and the talk of my balk.

They waited as I slated and I was tainted, but I never fainted, I only

soaked and poked.

Crazy and lazy, but with Daisy!

6-20-07   Mr. Bad

"Crazy and Lazy" is another poem written because I was aware of people spying and stalking upon me, along with their talk about me. I have had a daughter stalking me around and being involved with an Arab male, trying to tell the law, who also have been behind me, that I was crazy and even lazy. It seems as though there have been many people, who followed me around hiding behind trees, bushes, and buildings. There seems to be those, who attempt to keep lottery and sweepstake winnings from me, and those, who tried to get the winnings and a girlfriend to me. They have tried to mark me and even put shame upon me. They have followed me to all my places of employment watching me sweat and work hard, as they still attempted to say I was lazy.

Broken time Piece

A shiny 94 Beretta and clean as can be.
A smoke shack, but without a seed.
My sleigh was paid in cash and I could see.
Residence with a number and a deed.

The one and only operator with four wheels and a G.
A coach without Cinderella and a lost 14 carat winder of gold.
Fully functional, legal, stinging like a bee.
A slip and I got the tip; the detective must have been bold.

The broken time piece and my sole had no crease.
Upon polished holly laid lost and found.
Never had I rented and there was no lease.
I knew I was tracked by a hound.

The piece I knew came from the detective.
My wagon was dusted, but it was under my feet.
Broken time piece came to be reflective.
I was aware that it came from one on the beat.

Like a hand in the cookie jar laid that piece.
Monitoring service, which lost and gave a clue.
I didn't catch the name, but maybe it was Reese.
Now comes the time to pay their due.

6-21-07   Mr. Bad

This poem is a poem written about a wrist-watch winder I found in my Chevrolet Beretta, which I owned and operated. My car was kept clean most of the time and I never allowed others to drive it. I had sensed that I was being followed by the law because I started to hear their voices at places I went, such as shopping, school, and work. It became apparent to me that I was being followed by the law, after I found the wrist-watch winder made of gold on my front driver's side floor board of my car. I knew someone had their hand up in my dashboard and most likely got their watch-winder pulled out of their watch, as they attempted to pull their hand back out of the dashboard. I myself never wore a watch and no one else was in my car that had been missing one. This poem is therefore titled "Broken time Piece."

Water Only

The belly feels good when the crispy chicken is on the plate.

But when the plate is empty the ceramic doesn't satisfy.

The belly feels great when the red wine is with the date.

But when the wine glass is empty the polished glass doesn't ratify.

The belly feels good when the silverware has a fight.

But not when the shiny silver is without a stain.

The belly feels good when the salad is in sight.

But not when the green leaves with their toppings are not part
of the main.

The belly feels good when the desert is scrumptious.

But when the fruit salad is colorless you sure get rambunctious.

The belly feels wonderful when the mouth is full.

But when the taste-buds are frictionless the esophagus can't pull.

The belly feels great when it stretches in delight.

But when the prune is dried out the moisture has no route.

The belly feels abundance when the candles relight.

But when the flicker is out so is the scout.

The belly feels, as if there is a tomorrow when there is
something to eat.

But when the kettle is empty so is your right.

The belly feels very ill when there is water only.

6-22-07   Mr. Bad

"Water Only" is a poem written about a time I had while staying in a three bedroom house and I starved about a week straight with water only. I could hear the voices outside my house that were from the law, a young blonde girl, a daughter of mine, and others, as they pride upon my privacy, causing me mental stress and starvation. I can honestly say though, after having starved and survived the hard times, that when a person really starves that bad, the heartbeat can be felt in your stomach.

Looking for Mr. Goodbar

From the radio my ears were stretched like a feather.
The announcer was asking, if there is someone or whether.
Her name I was told was not Heather.
I am sure she would look good in leather.

Her name I was told was Sheri and she had been searching
for a sweet berry.
Requirements were given, but they did not ask for Larry.
I imagined a girl grazing in a pasture and a whole dairy.
I felt a little lucky and thought she was a good fairy.

She was looking for Mr. Goodbar and gold fingers, one who could
open her jar.
I didn't suggest, but said I searched for a gold bar.
Once I did take the bus because I had no car.
Of her residence I had no clue, near or far.

Her voice then was apparent to me, she chose me over the other one.
She started to follow and I had some fun.
I waited to see when she would knock and we would be done.
So, I wished that we would have a son.

Her presence was noted by me, not just once, but all the time.
She found her Mr. Goodbar and I wrote her a rhyme.
She hung on tight and she knew I had not a dime.
She was indeed young, but I committed no crime.

6-24-07   Mr. Bad

This poem was written about my young sweet blonde girl who follows me around. Her presence has been noted by me the whole time. She had been following me at the time of the making of this poem, about three years now, waiting for her father to allow her to just say hello to me. She has been freezing the last two winters hiding outside my house of residence and going through every summer night waiting for me. She was "Looking for Mr. Goodbar" and, therefore, is this poem so titled.

When she is Eighteen

There were the answers, which were not true.
There were the ones, who lied and turned blue.
There was the talk and I had more than a clue.
There was a first, a Japanese woman and I asked her to say, I do!

I played my hand of poker with a hand full of jokers.
I spun roulette, threw craps, and dealt with brokers.
I was the cook, baker, and bought from the best grocers.
I turned the table with players and swung with cokers.

I gave a promise that when she is eighteen.
I will drive, fly, ride, and with her take a freight-train.
I didn't know, but I learned she was just fifteen.
I said I would wait, until she is eighteen.

We want my blonde and me to be one for the other.
We want, me and many, even her brother.
We want her not to smother.
When she is eighteen she wants to be a mother.

When she is eighteen I'll take her to heaven and back.
When she is eighteen I'll take up all her slack.
When she is eighteen I'll be true and never lack.
When she is eighteen I'll let her be my nick-knack.

6-24-07   Mr. Bad

"When she is Eighteen" is a poem I wrote as I waited for a young blonde girl to be eighteen, who wishes to be with and marry me. Since my return from Germany in the year 2000 I have been making an attempt to be married once again. While I was attending the university I made an attempt to marry a Japanese woman who was my Japanese language instructor. The Japanese woman after consideration told me she had gotten married and I was also told that she returned to Japan. I then became upon a young blonde girl, Sheri, and at the time I thought she was twenty-three years old or so, but to my surprise she wasn't. I had promised her that I would wait till she is eighteen and give her a joyful and rewarding life with me. The women, the Japanese and the young blonde girl had been secretly following me around and spying on me. Whenever I asked if someone knew something about them following me, they said they knew nothing and that I must have a mental problem, even though I heard them talking behind my back.

Golden Fingers

A hand of five or two of ten.
They measure up to the greatest when.
A touch of this and a touch of that.
See what they have pulled out of a hat.

Fingers so line and they are mine.
I wish they could dine.
They are fingers of gold and not pine.
Golden fingers they are and they are so fine.

When they touch, they bring so much.
They are though, also a little Dutch.
Golden fingers they are and of such.
They walk the keys and need no crutch.

Fingers of gold and music they play.
They even write a special way.
Golden fingers, so I say.
They are for a very special day.

These fingers of mine, they are so gold.
They are so shiny, but they are not cold.
Like a mold of gold, they hold.
Golden fingers and they told.

6-24-07   Mr. Bad

"Golden Fingers" is a poem I wrote because as I was living alone in a three bedroom house, I had developed six songs on an organ I worked for using the hours of work to pay for it. It was the type of organ you would possibly find in a church with many buttons, along with its own drum beats. The music I created without learning to play either an organ, or a piano. Therefore, I like to think that I have golden fingers and have titled this poem as such. However, one of the songs is a new wedding song I wish to put on the market and play live at my next wedding. It is twenty-eight minutes in duration and compilation and it has a very wonderful sound to it and I call it Love Boat Alley. The music is like there are two tug boats pulling their freight towards each other and steps are built within the music for the steps the bride takes to the alter.

The Sharks and the Mermaid

Half fish and half beauty, she swims in a treacherous sea.
Her floral of fins and elegance is all that need to be.
She is a goddess and so sweet, like the honey from a bee.
She swims in the deep, but her territory is not free.

Pursuance is near, shadows in the deep, which she has to fear.
Approaching ever closer and soon the terror will be too near.
Sonic vibrations travel to her as she swims for the clear.
The predators near and with fright she can hear.

Swift and furious with razor fangs, the shadows become larger, as her
nerves begin to wither.
A path of wet and blue divides, as her perspiration is slither.
Dashing from the deep she swings her tail dither.
Frantically splashing the chaos explodes hither and thither.

Massive and mighty the fearless snap with an explosion and the fright is
too terrible.
She splashes to transcend the cold sweat that is unbearable.
The taste of a mermaid seems to be less than parable.
Opportunity becomes a delight and unintelligible.

Fin thrashes and water splashes, as freedom becomes frantic.
The sharks and the mermaid's fights are gigantic.
The escape is back deep in the Atlantic.
Out of the depth comes the strike of a dolphin, which sinks the sharks like
the Titanic.

6-27-07   Mr. Bad

"The Sharks and the Mermaid" was written to express how I can hear a certain girl trying to escape from being terrorized and molested with drugs from two male individuals, as she attempts to be with me and be free. Her father will not allow us to meet and greet one another, so she must fight the two male individuals off, even freezing out in the cold. I can always hear them in the distance and what is said outside in the open, as I am homeless myself sleeping outside and attempts are made upon her with drugs and sexual acts. For me it is very terrifying to hear how she must go through such tremendous harassment and terror.

God's Will

We are all creations of the mighty God.
At times I look in the sky above and nod.
What God may want, God will get.
At times he uses more than just his wit.

God is good and God is great.
God has the will like a huge freight.
God's will is the greatest thrill.
God has the will like the greatest hill.

Six days of wonder and even with the thunder.
From far above us and deep down under.
Creations of nations with the best notations.
God's will could be probation.

God is good and God is great.
God's will could give you the largest bill.
God gave the apple which Adam and Eve ate.
God's will is like the works of a mill.

God is heaven and God is earth, God is will of birth.
God's will has the greatest girth.
It is the will of God, which deserves a prayer and a nod.
God's will and the will of God.

6-27-07   Mr. Bad

This poem "God's Will" is a poem I wrote to express that it must be God's will for me to be together with, Sheri, the young blonde girl, who follows me wherever I go and is in love with me. Sheri, which is her given disc-jockey name, as she worked at a radio station. She is the young blonde girl, who is in my heart and much of the poetry I wrote. She follows me every step of the way, wherever I go and she waits to be eighteen so that she no longer is authorized to ask her father's permission to say hello to me. She spends the entire hot summers outside and also the very cold winters as well, following behind me waiting to say hello. Her father does not fully agree to our age difference but still I say it is God's will.

Operator 911

Operator 911 would you please connect my call!
Help is needed Mr. Bad shouts through the wall!
He's doing homework, he hollers, parties, and he has the ball!
Help help, he is starting to gnaw!

Yes yes, indeed I did shout and holler; maybe I caused one to call!
No no, I am not crazy, but maybe I may knock on the wall!
Yes yes, indeed I did smoke and play ball!
No no, I did not eat, but I started to gnaw!

Operator 911, it could be Dr. Jeckle, or maybe Mr. Hide!
Help is needed because Mr. Bad does not abide!
He's doing homework, he hollers, and parties on the other side!
Help help, maybe he died!

Yes yes, indeed it could have been Dr. Jeckle, or Mr. Hide!
No no, Mr. Bad shouted and did not abide!
Yes yes, he was doing homework on the other side!
No no, he never died!

The facts are clear and someone made the call!
It's true, Mr. Bad shouted through the wall!
Yes, I did have a great ball!
I am correct, but I never had to gnaw!

6-30-07   Mr. Bad

"Operator 911" was written because the facts seem clear to me, or at least, as I hear them, that someone had made a call to my daughter in Germany because I was yelling in the apartment complex in which I was living, or maybe it was the call I made myself. I was attending the university at the time and was always doing homework in the evening. I was also being followed by the law, or at least believed to have been and I was yelling because they were on my nerves, looking for whatever it was they were looking for, so I was yelling and angry. The whole scenario brought my daughter from Germany to my home town and as she began to follow me and she also got involved with other peoples bad doings and not saying hello to me, as she should have done, but instead caused a tremendous amount of pain, not just to me, but others also.

Mistaken Identity

There has been a secret whisper, which became much crisper.
There had been a shuffle, which also then became to be a ruffle.
There had been talk, which even started to be lisper.
There had been lies, which led to a scuffle.

So, it had been told that I was crazy.
Voices all around me, as I was told it was not true.
So, it had been told that I was even lazy.
People behind me, as I was told they had no clue.

There had been bad days in my life now used and abused against me.
There had been stalkers and government officials, who waited and
played games to see.
There had been the mistaken identity, as I listened and wanted to be.
There had been much pain caused to me, which was without Cree.

So, it had been told that those days have passed.
So, they followed, the rich and the poor, but did not come to my door.
So, it had been told that I should be gassed.
So, it had been told that starvation was caused and I even slept
on the floor.

The mistaken identity was of me and it caused a lot of pain.
The mistaken identity was of me and it caused loneliness.
The mistaken identity was of me and my mentality was twisted, as I
waited for the gain.
The mistaken identity was of me and they wanted to cause homelessness.

6-30-07   Mr. Bad

This poem "Mistaken Identity" was written like many others to express my sanity and the truth, before it is told, that I was well aware of people following me and causing a lot of grief. A daughter of mine told law officials and others that I was crazy and even lazy. The stalking behind me and rumors, along with stories told about me, had been detrimental and caused me loss of quite a few places of employment where I was forced to quit, as I tried to shake them off me. The stalking and the rumors not only caused a lot of non-beliefs but mental stress, loneliness, homelessness, and pain to me.

Hollywood's Finest

A charm indeed, but did you know she is mean?
Her voice came as a whisper, then it was throughout the scene.
She is alright at times and maybe clean.
Hollywood's finest and so lean.

She arrived with a bulge and then started to indulge.

Her wants and needs became apparent, as she searched for the one
to deed.
I wrote many rhymes and she started to read.
Shiny blue eyed with a flare, but she did not show care.
Long light brown hair with curves that need.
She stalked, walked, and talked, as she would dare.
Her fur became raised, as that of a bear when she started to feed.

Hollywood's finest and viewable at every checkout line.
Very well known and she had my children, which were grown.
She scratched like a cat and kicked like a mule to get mine.
Hollywood's finest rode that one great deer before she was thrown.

Her name was, and is done.

7-4-07   Mr. Bad

This poem "Hollywood's Finest" is a poem I wrote about a Hollywood actress, who must be in possession of my children and follows me around in search of a new husband. I have never met this woman, but I am aware of who she is because I hear her talking, as she spies upon me and others say her name. She is a Hollywood actress, who sits at award conventions and such in the front row, but for me to write her name it could be detrimental for her, so, it is hidden and not to be conveyed. A hint lies in the final line of this poem.

The Devils in Disguise

Swift with their tongues, as they spoke from the dark.
They told falsified stories of me, as they played their game.
At first there was the wolves' howl, but then came the puppy, which
couldn't bark.
They snooped with their pampers full of poopers, as they attempted
to be the same.

Shamefully in red with horns of a bull.
They attempted to manipulate, as God stood watching in the sky.
Guided and protected from the evils of darkness, God gave me my tool.
The time has come for the devil's goodbye.

Not one, but two these devils of mine.
They are like burning coals with fangs of phantoms.
They came to prey upon my women and thought they could dine.
Searching for the weak they wiggle with temper-tantrums.

To Jesus and God I sat and prayed for a hand out of the light.
I prayed that the goodness of grace would extinguish these devils in
disguise.
I know it has been written about the war between the dark and the light,
which was a great fight.
To God I prayed because the devil I despise.

The devils in disguise, as they lurk throughout the night.
With tongues of a serpent and eyes all white.
To God I prayed that they become a new site.
The devils in disguise are not alright.

7-4-07   Mr. Bad

This poem "The Devils in Disguise" was written by me because it seems I have two male individuals stalking behind my daughter and the young blonde girl I plan to marry, who also follows me. It seems that they attempt to manipulate truth, as they commit crimes such as; molesting a minor, felonious assault, criminal trespassing, drug trafficking, attempted rape, attempted vehicular homicide, drugging a minor, stalking, and many more crimes, as they attempt to withhold my young blonde lover from me for a Hollywood actress, who thinks I may want to share my riches with her. The two male Arab individuals pretend to be sheep, but are actually wolves and devils.

Mail Please!

A new spot on the block for me with a box.
A number on a street where I could be discreet.
A delivery station that was not on the docks.
A home of freedom and a place of my own, or for others to mistreat.

I began on the Internet and entered the sweepstakes all.
My spot with the box received letters that started to pile up more.
You won you won the envelopes stated and they started to call.
The entries and letters rose to a sum of many, as I started to adore.
Win this win that, enter this and enter that, so I did, them all.

I tallied them up in seven years to 69,000 plus.
A total value in prizes has risen to three hundred and sixty million
dollars and still I wait for the rest.
I won I won, but when do I empty the train, truck, or bus?
I have heard voices say that I have climbed to the crest.

Then came the suffocation, my fame must have been the best hit.
My letters with the wins had disappeared after the news station got the
fact sheets.
Now I search for help and ask, "Where is my little bit?"
I even played six tracks with my cheap beat.

Now I enter one hundred and eighty sweepstakes a day.
I wrote seven books, but cannot pay my stay.
Someone has thieved and sent my life astray.
Still, I wait to sit at the bay.

7-4-07   Mr. Bad

"Mail Please!" is a poem I wrote, after I noticed there was a disappearance of my mail. The disappearance was sweepstake letters, which I constantly received and they stated that I won a check for cash. At one time, about three years before the writing of this poem, I was receiving ten to twenty letters a day with the United States' postal system. The fact is that now three years later, as I have doubled and even tripled the entries awaiting one real prize, I received not one letter for the past three years now. I have contacted the government and postal system asking about the postal loss, but it seems no person is willing to be honest with me.

The rat's Delight

The rat has a name and he has his fame.

He has his dirty hole and he is out every night.

They say he has a bite and he is the one to blame.

He searches for a nibble, which might be in his sight.

The rat, he searches for the others' rest.

A crumble or a lost rotten piece of the others' delight.

Still they say that the rat is the best.

Lick upon and sniff around, the rat can be fright.

Moldy cheese or an old man's bread, he lives another night.

A rat has hunger, as he is forced to bite.

The rat's delight, he finds his right.

It is the fight, which brings the rat his dinner in the light.

They set the trap, they rap, and they gather together, it is the rat's delight.

The rat, he slips and slides, he finds his dinner on the other side.

The rat, his prayer, his prey, and he must recite.

The rat's delight is a dirty bite, but he has his rights, as he takes others

for a ride.

He snips and snaps, as he chews the others' wraps.

He creeps and he craws, but how will he feel after he naps?

The rat's delight, as he is chased to a new site.

The rat's delight is the best, alright.

7-8-07   Mr. Bad

"The rat's Delight" is a poem I had written because the intelligence of my hearing has informed me that there were male individuals attempting to manipulate and molest a young lover away from me. They have stalked behind me for some time now, like rats they attempt to nibble on my girlfriend, who is forced to wait until she can say hello to me. As she awaits our first meeting and the two male individuals act like rats and attempt to get droppings and rests that are behind me.

Sheri

A girl with a deep affection for me and her heart so strong.

Bleach blonde she is and so young and her love is not wrong.

Cute like a doll and all others say, "Wow!"

Divided by chaos from me she is, as others attempt to take a bow.

Each time I move from place to place her shadow is to hear.

From front to back she has nothing, which I need to fear.

God's work of art she is and she wants to be so great to me.

Help is all around her, as she fights to be free.

I too have the love for her, as I await her body and soul to see.

Just around the corner is a life for us both, as we wait to be.

Knights with shining armor could not fight, as I do for you.

Lengthy nights illuminate, as I wait for her too.

Moonlight shines while she progresses to be free.

Nothing can barricade her will to sparkle like a sea.

Over the greatest mountain tops she will travel to be what I seek.

Precious, as the gems upon her she will be, as she climbs to the highest peaks.

Queen of a dynasty you are and special to be.

Ritually you sacrifice from yourself and you always agree.

Systematically you deplete, but you never retreat.

Tomorrow will come and today will be gone, as you recreate.

Unanimously you receive the love I have to share.

Variety is for those with choice of care and for those who dare.

Waiting patiently we yearn for the others care.

X-ray extra, I can see how you have the flare!

Your love I feel and hear; it comes, as if I see so clear.

Zeros or a tear-box and the picture is so dear.

7-12-07   Mr. Bad

"Sheri" is a poem I wrote for my sweet young lover who follows me around waiting to be with me. This poem is written to express what she is to me and how I feel about her. The attempt was to rhyme starting each sentence using the entire English alphabet, A to Z. I have waited some time now for this young love of mine, Sheri, and she has grown very deep in my heart.

Freight Train

Loaded down with green freight and I carry mid-weight.
I write and I sorrow, as I fish with the best bait.
I dip and I dive, as I carry the greatest crate.
I wait and I holler for the nicest date.

Freight train and I ship the main.
I know bad days and I felt the pain.
I lift it and I load it with the tallest crane.
I lost and I have been followed, but I'll get the gain.

Stacked high and my train will know how to fly.
I don't take, I always buy.
I play God's game and even I cry.
They say I'm hi, but I'll never die.

The weight pulls the freight and there is no stopping till the cork is
popping.
I travel with the sweet because I have the beat and I'm the topping.
Freight train travels and there is no stopping.
I jump tracks and I'm hopping.

Freight train and I'm the main and even sane.
I travel in the sun and even the rain.
Freight of pain and I carry the main.
I have the weight and the gain.

8-9-07   Mr. Bad

This poem has been written, as I try to express the fact that I am unstoppable, but there is an attempt to deprive me of sweepstakes winnings I work so hard for and there is an attempt to withhold advancements from me in life. However, I search for a better life, one with more respectability and a little wealthier one at that, than my present status is providing. I have written seven poetry books, created music for two music compact disc, I have plans for a patent with an agreement contract, contracts on my books, a total time of poetry readings from my books for about seventeen poetry compact disc, along with, which is now became seventy-two thousand sweepstake and lottery entries with a total prize value of over three hundred and seventy million dollars. I have had people working against me to withhold my winnings from me, but books and music are a definite constitutional right, along with the capitalism, which is the United States' functioning system for wealth. This poem has, therefore, been titled "Freight Train."

Snapper Rapper

Like a great white buffalo he stands out.
With scars from dark nights the herd knows what he is about.
He leads a pack, he's a decorated scout.
Rap is a snap and he is never to doubt.
He is the kid on the block and he can travel like an astronaut.

Like a seed in the wind he came to create a new segment.
His words I could hear and the forces of an entire regiment.
Rapper and a snapper and he mends my ligament.
He brings me my bride, who will soon be pregnant.
With a warriors hand his color has the best pigment.

He's a cowboy and the kid on my block.
With his help and that from the Lord I shall receive my stock.
Snapper the rapper, he's a whip and a rock.
Indeed he came to mend and bring my ship to the best dock.
He's the leader of the greatest flock.
Like a soldier he is decorated and can remove any lock.
He's a snap with the best rap, as I wait with the tick tock.

9-24-07   Mr. Bad

"Snapper Rapper" is a poem written about a certain rapper we all call the Kid. He follows behind me warding off the two male individuals I have previously written about in other poems, along with a Hollywood actress who uses these two male individuals to manipulate things, so that she can have me and the riches I heard the government say I have. My friend the rapper, he snaps at these individuals, who hide behind me. He is there for me, as he persuades others that I am alright and worthy of my young lover, along with the wealth, which must be behind me.

Eyes on You

Whether by sunlight or moonlight the stage is set.

A rat's race and they all placed their bet.

They shouted and pouted, as I went in debt.

They amused and abused, especially when they were wet.

Whether by night or day there were eyes on you.

A woman's taste, as there were decisions made too.

I listened and I wondered, as there were eyes on you.

At times I had blushed crimson red, felt faint, and turned ghost-

white, but remained sad and blue.

Whether by rain, sleet, sun, or snow there were eyes on you.

A wealthy man's dream it was, as they followed and discussed

about me too.

There have been the voices and eyes on you.

They have cried, tried, and denied, but I remained true.

Whether there have been, or not I say, "Eyes on you."

They have had the sight and I was always right and now

I sing out too.

The choices of voices and they had their eyes on you.

Looking and looking, as I shouted out, "Who?"

Whether there were those who showed or glowed there will always be

those who know.

They tried to hide and did not abide in the dark like a black crow.

There were those who could flow and stay low, but the eyes

on you would know.

Eyes on you, even a doe or maybe Joe, but I did know.

10-15-07   Mr. Bad

A long time has been spent, as I have listened to people following me and discussing about me. They were not exactly sure, whether or not, if I was aware of the fact that I was being followed so I wrote all the poetry too. The poems are all dated to recall all the progress of a young blonde, who fought, starved, pained, grieved, froze, and even carried on insomnia for her right to be with the one she loves, me. The law was protecting her against other evil doers, who attempted to divide us the entire time and there was always someone watching, not only her, but me also. Therefore is this poem written and called "Eyes on You."

Our Hearts are True!

It has been some years now, as time has passed us.
The cheers and fears I have heard and even when she cried.
She loves me and I her too and our hearts and hands will join together
before we fly.
Like angels we prayed and preached for the other and this can never be denied.

We have waited and dated each day and night because our hearts are true.
We fight the spooks and rage war with the crooks, as we wait for the
words, I do!
Together we cover generations, but yet there are not two.
Together our hearts are true and they are only two, which always say,
"I love you too!"
Our hearts are true because they are those that ask not who.

The pride we share and we always dare.
Our love will shine because it is so fine.
We care and we share because we never need to beware.
Like glass and wax we have class and the Dax.
Our hearts are true because we love, care, share, dare, and are aware.

A promise was made within the shades and the poetics of life are laid.
She asked me kindly within her fright, so I answered, "I'll wait another night."
The mountains around us grew tall, the valleys so deep, and the rivers
current so swift we had to wade.
Members of her clan went lost and astray, as our adventure had its cost
and a day, as we counted suns and moons for our right.
Our hearts are true, they say, "I do!" and "I want you too!"

10-19-07   Mr. Bad

"Our Hearts are True!" is a love poem I wrote for my very sweet young blonde, who I love so much. She has followed me several years now for her right to be with me. I have always heard her say how much she loves me. We both have waged a war and a waiting game together to be with each other, as we search amongst friends to battle off others, who attempt to divide us, but our hearts are true. I had promised her once, as we spoke without the view or sight of each other that I would wait too. A great battle has been raged in order for her to be my wife because we love each other so greatly, regardless of our twenty-some years age difference.

Song Birds that Weep

The winter's blanket gives the view a soft touch.
It may be a little, or so much.
Near and far the camouflage decorates the scene.
Perforations were the same color, as was it all clean.

In winter the song birds sleep, so they say.

The fall is brilliant and vibrant, as the nuts and berries are collected.
The fruitful droppings lay scattered, as the song birds are elected.
With the wind the colorful knispers wisten, as they are pushed about.
Harems of beauty lay pageant, as the cold breeze puts the acrobats
on their route.

In the fall the song birds creep, so it is said.

The summer's bright skies and the blaze of bright light scorch the
early morning's dew and the short nights of darkness.
From and to cracks and crevices the birds carry sticks and straws and
that what may crawl into darkness.
The grass so green and the streams so clean, as life has its abundance.
The gathering of the prey and the prayer is for redundancy.

In the summer the song birds swim deep, so has it been told.

The spring's reflection rampages through the frost of many cold days.
The floral arrangements are in surplus, as the stage is set for new ways.
The song birds' orchestra strums, as new life appears before us all.

Mr. Bad

The song birds' song shall have a new call.

In the spring, the song birds will weep, so shall it be told and they shall not be so bold.

10-20-07   Mr. Bad

"Song Birds that Weep" is a poem written about how the seasons go by, as my young blonde angel fights against two male individuals, the song birds, who use drugs and fright to scare her away from me. It is believed by me that the young blonde girl shall be eighteen in January of 2008 and the song birds shall weep because of their defeat. Our plans are to be married and be together. We are in love.

Analyzation

It was said that, "People are free."
They could roam and wonder across the valleys and hills.
It's given by he or thee.
Some even try freedom with their Cree.

I waited and pondered at the sight.
The rights are given and taken without a pen mark.
I've listened and I've heard who is right.
Freedom is a wild fire from a spark.

The one girl is fighting because she wants a night.
Another is in starvation saturated with fats.
They all knew I'd lick, but never bite.
Two others I know who tip no hats and get only bats.

I've sat and gazed and thought about.
I've laid and had ways, even ought or not.
Gem, she tried to keep me on the same route.
She abused two others in order for her to find Scott.

The offices are moaning with jurors out of suit.
The scene is tragic and scarier with every night.
"Sunshine baby" must have drunk her beer in a boot.
"Two sneaks and no sheik" tried to unveil her in the fight.

The spectacles are parting and it is time for a breather.
The stress has mounted up to a lot.
"Sunshine baby" told the one, "Not either, but neither."
By sun and moon "Two freaks" were put on the spot.

Strip or strap, take and make, freedom is about to bake.

"My love for her" is very immense.

Will she make it before a trip is to take.

There are two, who use the pretense.

I write and wait, as I listen to all the hate.

I glare and histen, as I have to wait.

The stage is set with blonde bait.

I just won't be the second date.

10-27-07   Mr. Bad

"Analyzation" is a poem that was also written about my young lover, Sheri. Her attempts to be with me are tormented, as I listen not only in the day, but also in the night. I must add two and two together to get four by listening to their voices and analyzing what is being played out behind my back, as I sit homeless and try to figure out what is what. It seems as though, Sheri, is guarded and protected with help from the government, as we attempt to persuade others with our actions to allow us to be together and be married. I am at this point unable to work because I am being followed by so many people and my funds are kept below minimum status and life is really taking its toll, not only on me, but my lover, Sheri, as well.

For You

The song I made and it's just for you.
The music is a beat and a strum that is second to none.
With loving hands I wrote the poetry too.
The pages carry their weight of a ton.

Miraculous as it may be, it all came without a lesson.
From a bump to a thump my heart gave a beat with the heat.
My fingers created a curve for a different session.
A new path has been laid like the prairie covered with wheat.

For you only my dear because you have a special ear.
Your eyes will behold quadruple fold.
You are the one who I could never fear.
The love within the art could never be sold.

The creations are from heaven I'm sure you have been told.
My heart is filled with laughter and so much joy.
For you only my dear because you are so bold.
If ever I play you are my special toy.

The makings will bring for you all the green flakes.
The Gods have adjourned and your life shall be a treat.
If your future could grow on a tree you would need many rakes.
For you my love, as I wait to meet.

10-30-07   Mr. Bad

"For You" was written and intended, as a letter to my girlfriend, who was a disk-jockey at a local radio station 104.7 FM in Toledo, Ohio. I have created six songs on an organ without learning to play an organ and one of the songs I have created with the intentions for my next wedding. My plans are to play in the church in which we shall be married, as she walks down the isle to the sound of this created piece of art. I also have worked on numerous poetry books, which I intend to publish.

Battle-lines

A story of a great fight.
A story of a chaotic route.
Not only in the day, but also in the night.
I'm given a tough bout.

Bush-whackers and those of crackers.
Divided by lines that always get so fine.
Followed by evil and backers.
The fight rages on, as I wait to dine.

A young trophy, which is forced to be done.
Two sneaks, who stand behind bushes and trees.
The other from the hills of Holley, who they say is second to none.
Dark Princess was molested by the others' Cree.

Battle-lines and the seasons go by.
Will she give in or must she is the question of time.
There were even times when I had to cry.
I already wrote so many different rhymes.

Battle-lines go east and west.
Pain and defeat, but a time must be met.
Homeless and I listen to fields of a different nest.
They even give a holler and place a bet.

11-5-07   Mr. Bad

This poem was written about a great struggle I have been having. It is a struggle to get a young blonde girl, who is in love with me. This young blonde girl has fought for her right to be with me. She is seventeen and she waits, either to be eighteen or for her father's permission to allow us to communicate and be with each other. In her process of defeating the Japanese language instructor, who was my teacher and named, "Dark Princess", she has struggled against a daughter of mine, who claimed I was crazy and unfit for a better life. Amongst this blonde girl's battle were two Arab male individuals named, "Devils in disguise", who attempted to molest and scare her away from me, while Gem, a Hollywood actress, attempted to steal me and bribe others with a million dollar check for cash, which she, as I heard claimed using my name for Micropuff's lottery on the Internet.

Her battle using the law and Snapper Rapper, the kid and rapper to ward off the evil doers has been from what my hearing tells me, a fierce battle to be with me. I fully respect all that the young blonde, Sheri, has done to help me and I love her deeply. May God bless her to the bone. This poem is therefore titled, "Battle-lines."

Heaven or Hell?

They say it was Heaven and they say it was Hell.
They say it is for always and never undone.
They say it was Heaven, but which one had the yell?
They say it is forever until one is none.

Heaven or Hell? Heaven or Hell?

They sat it was Heaven and then the darkest of one.
They say it was Heaven for them that can tell.
They say it is for them of the sun.
They say it is eternity and be so well.

Heaven or Hell? Heaven or Hell?

They say it was Heaven and they say it was Hell.
They say it is for always and never ending.
They say it was Heaven, but who had Nell?
They say it is becoming and always sending.

Heaven or Hell? Heaven or Hell?

They say it was Heaven for those sick or well.
They say it is for tomorrow and till the end of time.
They say it was Heaven, or was it Hell?
They say it is whether so I wrote a rhyme.

Heaven or Hell? Heaven or Hell?

They say it was Heaven with the golden gates.

They say it is Hell, or for those who are not to tell.

They say it was Heaven, or which one rates?

They say it is for those, who like to yell!

Heaven or Hell? Heaven or Hell?

They say it was Heaven and I ought not to sell.

They say it is chosen from second to none.

They say it was Heaven, or was it Hell?

They say it is Heaven and I'm done.

11-6-07   Mr. Bad

This poem I have written to express how it may be when the time comes and our destinies are chosen for us, or rather and perhaps made by us. Whether it will be heaven in which our eternity shall be chosen, or hell? As humans we are never quite sure, until the time has come, and likely others will never know either in which dimension they will be sent. Our faith guides us through life with the beliefs of a wonderful place in which we will be angels and be full of joy. For some it may be their actions in life, which could possibly lead them to the dimension of hell where there is, as has been told, pain, suffering, and flames of eternal burning, where people yell. Our future is, nonetheless, chosen from god. This poem is titled "Heaven or Hell?" to reflect this.

Freedom!

Oh, it's my freedom!

That brings me Eden.
From the top of a mountain or a valley below.
I'll travel around so free without a decoy.
Oh, it's my freedom!

Whenever I want him.
He'll always be my freedom.
Like the sun and the moon.
The stars in the night.
Oh, it's my freedom!

I paid high dues and took no I owe yous.
I sing it happy and I sing it sad.
Oh, it's my freedom!

From the sweetest waters and the wildest wines.
He'll always be my freedom.
The sun it shines and the moon is so bright.
I feel the breeze like a summer night.
He's the love that I have in sight.
I fought for him and he's my right.
Oh, it's my freedom!

He's the one that I'm dreaming of.

11-6-07   Mr. Bad

"Freedom!" is a poem, which was also intended to be a song for, Sheri, my young lover, who follows me around secretly and wishes to be a singer. I wrote this poem in hopes that someday she will do something with it and create a song from it and sing it to me. Her dreams are in search of a helping hand and someone, who can help her to fulfill her dreams.

Broken Record

"Pop tart thief" lingers on.
He's a real fine stalker looking for the steal.
I heard it was Mickey and not Don.
He comes with the substance and his abuse looking for a deal.

The same questions arise over and over.
Scratch, nick, and a pang come from my head.
Generosity was given, as I hold a four leaf clover.
"Blonde and beautiful" she is, but she needs to get to bed.

The same questions arise again and again.
Screech, pop, and a ding come from my head.
They told him it was Jesus and not a Sin.
Broken record is to read.

The same questions and I hear him cry.
At a distance he is a thief to wonder.
The same is also answered, bye-bye.
A broken record and then there is thunder.

The same questions he asks.
One more time.
He should have found other tasks.
Broken record is a rhyme.

Ping, zing, scratch, and wong it's a song.
He keeps trying for her thong.
We all know that broken record is wrong.
Snap, crackle, and pop, but stop the record it's long.

11-9-07   Mr. Bad

"Broken Record" is a poem written about a certain male individual, who attempts to steal my girlfriend behind my back. He seems to always ask the same questions in the distance, evidently not knowing that I listen about why he cannot have the girl who is in love with me. The quoted titles are previously written poems, which I had written about this male individual and my girlfriend "Pop tart thief", "Sheri", and "Blonde and beautiful." They would need referring to for the reader to completely understand the message I am trying to convey to them.

Wicked Witch from the West

"Gem" and "Blue sparkle", so I wrote.
She came, however, for my note.
Still "War of the women" rages on tremendously.
I await ones independency.

Wicked wicked and the witch is from the west.
Mirror mirror on the wall is she really the best?
Wicked wicked witch without a nest.
Still my wings will take me to the crest.

The creation plus nine ailments, two liars, nineteen moon disk, and the luck.
My dice are silver and sometimes gold.
I play "The game" with the largest buck.
My hands can be ice cold.

Wicked wicked and the witch is from the west.
Mirror mirror on the wall is she really a pest?
Wicked and not the best guest.
She surely is on the greatest quest.

She pushes and she pulls and she jerks with her curves.
"Who is she?" remains unknown and I'm blown.
A jitter has gotten to my nerves.
"Good-fairy" a secret "Blonde and beautiful" and she's grown.
Wicked wicked and the witch is from the west.

11-10-07   Mr. Bad

"Wicked Witch from the West" was written to express my feelings towards what seems to be a Hollywood actress, who attempts to divide me from a young lover of mine. The two girls are fighting for me, as the Hollywood actress uses two male individuals to divide us. The quoted names of titles are poems written in previous books, Poetic Shades of Life 1, 2, and 3. They would have to be read to fully understand what I am entirely trying to say.

Land of Eden

Land of enchantment it seems and land of the gigantic.
Where the people are simple and there are those with their dimple.
Where the fruits and berries are free, as they hang so huge like the
Titanic.
Land of Eden and those without a nimble.

A land of mossy green valleys and mountains with the greatest enhancement.
Where the sweetest and clearest waters flow and the purist grow.
Where plant life has its abundance and animals of unknown species roam
the embankment.
Where geography is still to be known with its oceans that lie so low.

Where the skies twinkle like a new born baby's eyes.
Where birds are of the enormous and they sound with the most tremendous
cries.
Where fish are of a million species, as they prey.
Where travel is slow and places remain non-adventured for a stay.

Where the forest seems vast and enchanted and love has a new day.
Land of Eden and the land of everlasting beauty.
Where the time will pass from primitive to a new way.
Where mankind once again must do his duty.

Land of Eden, where solitude is even.

11-15-07   Mr. Bad

"Land of Eden" was written in reference to a dream I had about being in some prehistoric land. There was a valley in which I was with mossy green coverage and two sorts of apple trees with apples on them. There was one sort of apples, which were as we have, but perhaps 6 inches in diameter. Then there was another sort of apples, which were two feet in diameter and, as I tried to carry them they were just too heavy. One spectacular thing was though when I arrived it must have been harvest season because I stood looking at the apple trees and the apples all fell from the trees at the same moment. The people were somewhat primitive and I was at what seemed to be a washing station and some people even had money, which was lying next to them, as they did their washing duties. The dream was very short, but spectacular, so I wrote this poem.

Hamster in a Cage

The crisp fresh straw is spread out in his cage.
The fresh water bowl has its place for his old age.
The hamster food is rationed, as they read the next page.
Hamster in a cage and he is so beige.

Hamster in a cage, but do you think he has rage?

The little sleeping house in the corner is for his stay.
The tiny little running wheel is pointed just the right way.
The cute old hamster was found at the bay.
Hamster in a cage and he looks at you every day.

Hamster in a cage, but do you think he is okay?

The transparent tunnels are placed in his cage.
The carrots and potatoes are given to him for his old age.
The thermometer reads just right, as they read the next page.
Hamster in a cage, which is made with the wrong gauge.

Hamster in a cage, but do you think he has rage?

The waste is always removed from his cage.
The fresh water is always replenished for his old age.
The hamster food is rationed, as they read the next page.
Hamster in a cage and he is so beige.

Hamster in a cage, but do you think he is okay?

The little sleeping house is moved for his stay.

The tiny wheel is pointed just the right way.

The old hamster should be released at the bay.

Hamster in a cage and he looks at you every day.

Hamster in a cage, but do you think he has rage?

They removed the straw from his cage.

They emptied the water, which was in his cage.

They no longer refilled the food in his cage.

They removed the wheel that was in his cage.

The hamster in the cage is no longer beige.

Hamster in a cage, but do you think he is okay?

11-20-07   Mr. Bad

"Hamster in a Cage" is a poem written to express how I feel about myself, after being stalked and talked about behind my back, as if I was a terrible person. The feelings are that everything is given in a polite manner to satisfy me and my needs, but then also directly taken from me. Like a hamster in a cage, I feel as though others sit and stare at me constantly, as if the cage is placed directly for their view upon me. It seems that others attempt to say that I am abnormal or mentally ill and put pain and anguish upon me. It is no wonder that I would not feel alright.

A long Wait

Three years now have been the making.
The fight has been so furious and I'm still waiting.
Once again the leaves I am raking.
I go fishing and I am still baiting.

Guardian angel named, "Snapper rapper."
"The win" is so green, as they are so mean.
I know they listen, but who is the taper?
I hear she is so cute and just a teen.

"Stalker's pride" will not override.
It has been a long wait, as I start to hate.
I wait and wait on the other side.
The wish is for just one date.

"Jesus" and "Dear God", did the Pope read about the cod?
Abide and take a side, when will the truth come, about who died?
On the other side they say who is odd.
I sit and listen and I know who cried.

Please Lord hear my plea.
A long wait I had indeed.
Please Lord I have my Cree.
A long wait I had in thee.

11-21-07   Mr. Bad

This poem "A long Wait" is a poem I wrote to say that I am aware of the fact that a young blonde girl has been following me around, as I also await for her to be eighteen years of age and free. She is at war with one woman from Hollywood, who seems to also be trying to get next to me and be my wife, until the end of my time. The young blonde girl is protected night and day by Snapper Rapper, a rap singer, who is well known and stays with her to protect her from two men, one Palestinian and another Jordanian, who seem not to be alright in their heads. They try to break us apart for this woman from Hollywood who is an actress.

The win is a poem written in one of my other published books and represents money I had won in sweepstakes from around the world. Stalker's pride is a poem, which also was previously written in Poetic Shades of Life 2 and represents the fact that a daughter of mine thinks she is being a good person by following me around and attempting to have a bad marking put on me, as a very ill person, which in my point of view is not the fact. Jesus and Dear God are also two previously written poems, which I wrote and had sent to the Pope in Italy.

Homeless

Like the third event of my life, I strengthen my own.
As I walk the streets of home, I'm known.
Like blades of grass in the wide open, I'm blown.
My future lie without a home, but I'll be grown.

Free like the stars that sparkle in the sky.
A wish will be made upon the stars that fly.
Like the sun and the moon, I could travel so high.
Homeless I am and I hope I do not die.

Homeless and domeless and sometimes even combless.
My path is laid, but it is stoneless.
Eternity shall be mine, but boneless.
My ways are free and zoneless.

God shall be my guide and I will abide.
I search to find a friendly side.
At times I must ask for a ride.
I swing and sway, like the ocean's tide.

The steps I take, until I find my way.
God is the only, who may say.
I search and search for my bay.
Homeless, but someday.

11-24-07   Mr. Bad

"Homeless" is a poem I have written about being homeless for the third time in the last five years, from the years 2003-2007. It has been written, as I was in a rehabilitation center for a short time because of mental stress and depression that was caused by being followed by individuals, who will not tell the truth. This poem expresses that I feel and travel so free, as I go from place to place under the skies of God and try to find a way to rid myself, of those who have been following me, better said, spying and stalking upon me. I await the pressure upon me to subside and a better life to come for myself.

Sunset

When the sun sets we remember the moments it rose so many times before.

We remember our thoughts and all the things that ought.

When the sun sets we remember the days before and all that we adore.

We remember the beauty from the day before and the memories it brought.

The sunset, its shadow distinguishes the life at store.

The sunset, its glow in the sky is a shows next act.

The sunset, its opening scene is never a bore.

The sunset, its Beaumont is beau and that is a fact.

When the sun sets we know our love for life and we respect.

We feel the light, as it transposes into the night.

When the sun sets it is to becalm and not to reject.

We see it soar with its roar and it's the greatest flight.

The sunset, it provides for a peaceful new night.

The sunset, it brings the night over the day and a new bright.

The sunset, it's a majestic site and a singe for a new sight.

The sunset, its birth is its calm for a newborn dawn's right.

When the sun sets we remember those who are in our hearts.

When the sun sets there are those who give us a new light.

When the sun passes the horizon we await for it to come like new darts.

When the sun has set we wait for a new bite.

11-29-07   Mr. Bad

This poem "Sunset" was written to express how great it is to be alive, even if a person is not having the most wonderful life. I have written this poem, along with others, as I had a short stay for rehabilitation from mental stress and depression, along with the tricks that were played against me. The sunset is a beautiful thing and at times we look back to the past, or the day that is ending and try to enjoy it. Life really is beautiful and all people should be proud to be part of it. It is when life ends like the sunny day when the sun sets that we can discover just how important life can be.

Fact or Fiction?

True indeed, but will people really believe?
I tried to tell and at times I had to yell.
The voices were real, as I looked for someone who would relieve.
I looked for progress, but got a lot of Hell.

I heard them say, as it came my way.
Fact of fiction, fiction or fact?
Sunshine Baby had to wait another day.
She followed me every step and played another act.

Fact or fiction, but was it addiction?
I heard them say, as it came my way.
Fiction or fact, fact or fiction?
Another tried to take me to her bay.

Non-fiction, but affliction.
I heard them speak, as it came my way.
Fact or fiction?
Another tried to say.

It was not fiction, but fact.
I heard them speak, their voices came my way.
They played yet another act.
I had to listen and say okay.

12-1-07   Mr. Bad

This poem "Fact or Fiction" has been written to express that I am aware of a young blonde girl following me, as I ask others, who have been aware, but have only told lies to me and said they were not aware and knew nothing of it. A daughter of mine has been abused, beat, and mistreated, as a Hollywood actress tries to divide me and the young blonde using two male individuals, as her helpers and the law watches, as I listen to the facts of their voices.

The time is Coming

Day of a Jew and now I started something new.
I traveled across the sea to sting like a bee.
They followed to explore and they have stalked me too.
There are those that have no Cree.

Time goes by, as I anticipate the change.
I sit and wait for the one I love.
Still there is an attempt to deny, as I get in range.
War of the Women and one must be above.

A daughter of mine with her sour wine.
She tries to stop the legend of my time.
I try to marry and go to dine.
She has committed the most awful crime.

A new era is dawning.
The sun will shine, as they are crawling.
The tears no longer run through the awning.
There are those who are sprawling.

Which will be?
I know, but can't wait to see.
I always heard the others say, "Gee."
Still there are those who agree.

12-3-07   Mr. Bad

This poem "The time is Coming" is another poem written, as I sit and wait for one of two women, who have been following me around to say hello. A daughter of mine has told law officials and others that I am crazy, so I have been having a very difficult time, as I wrote this poem. The titles are previously written poems. Day of a Jew is from Poetic Shades of Life 1 the first book written by me, War of the Women is about the two women, or now three to four, who follow me around and is also from Poetic Shades of Life 1 and, Which will be is from this same book and is a poem about, which girl or woman will get me and the new wedding song I have created and I will be playing it live, if all goes well.

Play it my Way

Play it, don't say it, do it my way.
I have seen good-times and I have seen them bad.
I matured with the roughest rounds and I heard them say.
They call me Chief, Doctor, Lawyer, and sometimes Dad.

I've seen them stun and I've seen them with a gun.
There is no chilling, it's all but filling.
I play my hand and it's all fun.
Play it my way, if you are willing.

I'll be all nice, drink tonic and Gin with a slice.
I ran with the beauties, mostly though they were cuties.
I play the poker hand and I toss the dice.
I arrive on time and I keep to my duties.

I Puff and I cuff, I hit like Tyse.
I raffle and I baffle, I take a hit of ice.
They come to hear me rhyme and it's all nice.
I write a book or two, play a song for you, I let them pay the price.

I carry the greenest dollars, as I give them a holler.
I don't jive; I sting like a whole bee hive.
My suits are plaid and pin striped, my shirts the whitest collar.
Play it my way, don't take no jive.

12-6-07   Mr. Bad

"Play it my Way" is some rap poetry, which I have written and it is humorous to me. I have sat homeless and listened to rumors about me and the dirty little tricks, which have been played in my vicinity. I am aware of what has been played and it has inspired me to write this poem. There are those who want to help, but seem not to get the job of eliminating two male individuals from harassing my young girl friend and my daughter finished. I just think they should be a little rougher and not be so softies, as they become attitudes towards these two individuals.

Not your Supreme?

Nacho Supreme and I'll be your best dream.
Margarita was last night, but still I put up a fight.
The best on the block with the hot sauce and cream.
A Chalupa with my beams, two tacos and a delight.

Like I am sitting wave side with my day tide.
The temperatures keep falling and I'm loud calling.
I sit and listen; I watch who has the best ride.
Two idiots, but I'm not falling.

Bean Burritos, Nachos, and Cheetos, Snickers, and Fritos.
I sit with my pride, I abide, and I let others decide.
Palestinian and Jordanian, two with the creepos.
I asked for no lies, but still I was denied.

Mama Seta and Fajitas, if I could jump on a Cheetah.
I sit with my pride even though others have cried.
A large soft wink, as I ask for Anita.
Beef on the side, I'd like it deep fried.

The sun and the moons, I look like Daniel Boone.
I sit with my dream; I got the cream and the team.
I wait for my girl and it will be real soon.
Like Betsy Ross, I sew my seam.

12-7-07   Mr. Bad

"Not your Supreme?" is a poem I have written while I sat homeless in a truck during the winter months without a key or heat. It was inspired by a Taco store, a Mexican fast food restaurant that was direct adjacent to my location where I stayed. Its message is that I feel myself to be a great person even if at the time it didn't seem so. The game is still being played around me, as a Hollywood actress is using two Arab male individuals to scare and chase, along with molest a young blonde girl, whose heart is set to be with me. I hear them argue a lot and even at times they cry. The situation is very touching and has me yelling out loud at times. American to the heart, as I am, I write and pray that dreams will come about.

The Unknown

My memories I keep in my thoughts, all material things have been
blown.

My past is the unknown, but still they say it has been shown.

My future can be read in those that have known.

My chessboard has the strategic move of which is my own.

My life, or past that I have created has a moan.

My joys are numerous and of a king's throne.

My happiness is sad, but never alone.

My serenity is the unknown.

My wisdom is knowledge; it is the facts that have grown.

My tongue speaketh when asked, like an angel that has been a clone.

My truth is the words I speak when I have glown.

My trust is golden, it is a loan.

My respects are given to those that have shown.

My movements are agile and lead to the zone.

My adventures are a path made of stone.

My love is the unknown.

My women are fragile like glass when it is blown.

My poetry is a mission, it is God's own.

My words are ancient when I am alone.

My name is the unknown.

12-7-07   Mr. Bad

This poem "The Unknown" was written, as a note to the facts that part of my past has been reinvented for me and an attempt has been made to burden me with it. Judicially it is not possible, corrupt, and also not correct, and the attempt to burden me has caused much grief and displacement upon me. As I attempt once again to have a female partner in life. This burdening has created difficulties for me and has cost me a lot of lost time. Still I remain with my faith in God and wait for the future to unfold.

Home

The days of the past with the kitchen all clean and the carpets all steamed.

The living room decorated with memories upon the walls.

The bathroom smelling fresh and the drains all streamed.

The dining room with its shiny table and the dust that occasionally falls.

A place to call home, where there is peace and love.

The shiny paned glass, the decorated doors, and a place where there is more.

A place with meaning and all of the above.

Where family joins and friends are to rely on to the core.

Home, such a pleasant feeling.

Something to be proud and happy of.

A place where God hangs above the ceiling.

A place with the resemblance of a white dove.

12-8-07   Mr. Bad

"Home" is a poem, which was written to say that, as I sit homeless for the third time in the forty-six years of my life, I too have had once before material properties and a happy family with all the dwellings that are inclusive with a nice life. At the time of writing this poem I, however, am poor and without much of anything. I am tormented and pressed to poverty and I do now realize even more how sweet a home is, after being homeless and without anything.

When the Truth Comes About

My life was pleasant at one time or another.
I was respectable, loyal, free, and without a doubt.
The seasons came and went, I always had a lover.
It was life in the fast lane, me being the scout.

Then came harshness, life had its other side.
The winds raged, lightning struck, life was a buck.
Mountains crumbled and the sea changed its tide.
Life became a bad dream and I didn't give a f . . . .

Darkness set in and my dreams were stuck.
My loved ones left me and a new future was to abduct.
I flew with one wing like a wounded duck.
Terror was on me and it all seemed to obstruct.

The sun never rose and the moon didn't shine.
I knew I was tainted and the past had a new route.
Awareness was present and the hill had its decline.
My life was changing, I had no doubt.

Hard times were upon me and I met my match.
Visibility became to near and my outlook was of grace.
I stopped to ask another how he could catch.
It seemed as though I had a new face.

They came to talk of the disgrace.
They coated me with rumors not knowing my past.

My life changed and I was tormented with my misplace.

I created a whole new cast.

Then came about the possibilities, which were unstoppable.

I learned and I yearned because heaven had its place.

My life developed the improbable.

God lent a hand and I had a new case.

There were those with their help and those I had to reject.

I was climbing the highest mountain about to reach the crest.

Developments were in me and life would reflect.

My future lies abreast.

The facts about me never arose.

The talk was created without the facts, nor my pose.

I sat waiting and froze.

I'd rather had been playing a set of Bose.

The truth shall come about me and my prose.

The lies will dwindle behind me, as I have rose.

When the truth comes about.

I'll be the best scout.

12-8-07   Mr. Bad

"When the Truth Comes About" is another poem written to express how things have been told about me and rumors spread. It tells that the goodness about me never came fully into the light and I was, nevertheless, obstructed with falsifications and saturated with lies about me, as mostly bad things were said about me. I have had a bad time in my life and it seemed that the sun had never risen. This short span of difficulties seems to be for some my life's entire story. After this bad time, which was in Europe, I have now joined my father and motherland once again, as was before my not so terrific span of life and have progressed with books and music, along with many sweepstake entries across the world. It seems as though there were winnings that were kept from me, monetary and material things, which have added to a harsh life for me. The truth, however, shall come about and the good things about me and my life shall come into the picture for others to see and hear.

She is an Angel

She is the one with a caring heart.

She is the one, who stays close every night.

She is the one with a soft voice and she is a sweet tart.

She is the one, who helps and is right.

She is the one with love that fills a cart.

She is the one, who is so innocent in my sight.

She is the one with loving arms and aims with her dart.

She is the one, who brings joy and shines so bright.

She is the one with talent and so smart.

She is the one, who is watching at every site.

She is the one with the goods like a mart.

She is the one, who has that special bite.

She is the one with her very special part.

She is the one, who I wish to squeeze so tight.

She is the one with the sparkle and very zart.

She is the one, who I love as I write.

She is the one with a remarkable art.

12-9-07   Mr. Bad

This poem "She is an Angel" was written for, Sheri, the young sweet girl, who follows me around waiting to be eighteen years old and join me with my plans for the future. This poem expresses thoughts and feelings I have for her and how she attracts me. To me she is like an angel because she helps me with my legal matters over things that have been written about, which are my winnings of sweepstakes and lotteries. This poem is also written with every other sentence containing either, one who, or one with.

In the Night

When the sun sets low and the lights show.

As silence controls the scene and they get really mean.

Like flowers they slowly start to grow.

I sit and listen to discover, who will be the queen.

Like mice they crawl in and out of their holes.

Quietly, they slip by to nibble in the night.

Patiently waiting I sit upon hot coals.

Sparingly, their voices can be heard in the night.

Like bats with fangs they fly by.

Blood-thirsty and terror for my ears.

In the night and at times I hear a cry.

The show is for my fears.

Silently like ants they crawl about.

Like a motion picture without the light.

Their faces cannot be seen, but they have a route.

They send chills through my spine and they have a great fight.

In the night there are those who gander.

They creep and crawl, as they have a great sprawl.

To expose the trees grain I need a sander.

In the night they crawl.

12-09-07   Mr. Bad

This poem "In the Night" was written about the nights of terror, as I sit homeless in a truck. I have been given the rights of use and stay out of the snow and wetness, as I still feel the winter's chill. My young lover is still behind me and accompanied by her father and others, as she is terrorized by two males previously written about. This young lover has had another, a Hollywood actress, who attempts to divide us and take her seat with me at my throne. The nights are filled with their voices, as she is molested and one of the male individuals attempts to persuade her father into allowing her to be wedded with him, so that the Hollywood actress may stop to play her role.

Day of Victory

A long journey has been voyaged to get to the day.
Like a stampede in the dust the clouds roar.
A cowboy's adventure with a cowgirl on the way.
Like John Wayne and Billy the Kid, I soar.

I found the one, who is deep in my heart.
She is to me like beauty of a queen.
A girl, a charm, one who shall never part.
Like a diamond she sparkles, her clarity is clean.

An angel, a Miss, and a shine so bright.
One in a million, a heart of gold.
Eyes that twinkle, shine, and glow just right.
Hands and heart I wish to behold.

The day shall come and we will join.
The heavens will open and our day will be done.
We shall have victory at the toss of a coin.
We'll have children and even a son.

The day of victory shall come.
God will grant us our right, after the fight.
Our hearts will pound and we'll be some.
In the eyes of the Lord we'll be together all night.

12-09-07   Mr. Bad

"Day of Victory" was written to say that after the harsh times I currently am going through subside, I will be joined with a female, who has, as I also have been, fighting to be joined and get married. It will be as the title expresses, our day of Victory over hard times we are having. She has fought for her rights to be with me and she has fought for my legal rights, along with my constitutional rights. We shall defeat the attempts against us to be free and we will join hands and hearts forever.

The Government

Time is of essence, but for those who don't care.
From the oval office down to those who don't share.
I've seen a lot of green and I've raised a hair.
They tell me don't do it, but I dare.

They took every dollar and dogged me to the bone.
They watched and followed me; they tried to turn me to stone.
I had a few licks and got down to the cone.
I am the king and I will have my throne.

The government office followed me wherever I went.
I kept up my emails and I told them it was sent.
They kept on driving and I got me a dent.
Money is all wonderful, but when it is not spent?

You can get, but you can't keep.
At times you have to weep.
They tried to smother and cover me as I had to creep.
You must swim to the rim when the water gets deep.

Govern and from above.
At times I even got a shove.
I was only asking for the peace of a dove.
Govern, but show me some love.

12-19-07   Mr. Bad

This poem "The Government" is a poem written because of my sense of hearing. I heard that the government was spying upon me and their voices were clear. I had many letters in the United States' postal system, declaring me as a sweepstake's winner and I had many letters in my emails saying that I was a lottery winner. My seventy-two thousand entries, which I had did make it very possible and clear to me that a possibility really did exist. I had contacted the government and I asked the postal system personnel to look into my loss of mail and after I contacted the media; the postal letters came to a halt.

It had been apparent to me because of the voices and things I was hearing, along with my loss of mail, that the government was investigating my legitimacy of the winnings and whether or not I was fit to receive them. The time of writing this poem is a time of being homeless and still I wait for answers to my claims for a better life, a legal one.

CSI

Like the Miami heat her voice is a hot whisper.
In search of love her face was in the picture.
I zoomed in and she was even crisper.
Like a ceiling's light she became a fixture.

A fourth in a row with a column of none.
The beauty on the screen and she is so lean.
To remain a friend when the game is done.
She is of beauty and she came to the scene.

The clock gave a tick tock and she was on my block.
With flare and care she came and she really did dare.
Her presence was noted, as she approached the dock.
Precious like gold she is so rare.

On Monday nights when the show begins.
My eyes begin to sparkle and I put on a happy grin.
To no other could she be twins.
To the crime scene she came.

She is to me like a dolphin with the shiniest fin.
The criminals and defenseless were the main.
She wanted to investigate, but it was not the same.
The possibilities were the gain.

12-20-07   Mr. Bad

This poem is yet of a fourth woman, one who I actually invited for a date. She, like blue sparkle or gem, comes from Hollywood to be a friend, or possibly much more. The only problem is that I am already involved with one other so she is not authorized to even say hello until my sunshine baby becomes old enough to be in the line-up, when I am to choose between the one that is to be my wife and the others, who may remain friends, or not.

The fourth woman will maybe be offered a business opportunity in which she may read poetry for a percentage of profits onto poetry compact discs. Her friendship I'm sure will be most pleasant and enjoyed, as the future evolves. The time until the choosing is estimated at the time of this poem, to be within one month. Because this fourth woman comes from a television crime scene show, which is called, "CSI", therefore, is the title so.

I'll Knock for You

Out of the deep of the jungle they secretly approach.
Maybe barefooted with swords, I don't know.
Their silent footsteps I heard and they were not in a coach.
Their voices were apparent, like a brilliant glow.

They followed me for the longest and they have seen that I am the strongest.
With quarrels and their heart aches they have shown.
I, like them too have waited the longest.
The young blonde, as they have been told is grown.

The chaos involved must come from the unintelligible.
From the weepings to the creepings I collect the rest.
Like journeys of a thousand places it is all unimaginable.
They stalk and they talk, as they say I am one of the best.

Like the phantom of the opera and Frankenstein live I wait for a knock.
Choices have been made and the weird are astray.
I'll knock for you, as I look upon the clock.
It has been a long wait and even love has gone away.

With a stick, a rock, or with a knuckle I wish they would knock.
I can't keep counting the clock.
It is known everywhere on the block.
I'll knock for you because it's time to buy some stock.

12-24-07   Mr. Bad

This poem has been written on Christmas Eve and was written because of hardship caused to me. To my knowledge I have a young blonde following me, along with two Hollywood actresses, the government, my daughters, a rapper, who is well known, and many friends. The young blonde girl has helped me to become my lottery and sweepstake winnings through the use of the government, who to my understanding has money of mine collected, but is tied up in legal questions about me. The young blonde, Sheri, the one I have been writing about is a young lady, who wishes to be and should be my wife. The two movie stars, of which one I invited for a date and recording contracts, the other who is in possession of a million dollar check and a new vehicle I won in a lottery over the Internet from Micropuff has also been tailing me around and waiting for the government to authorize them to say hello because they must wait for the young blonde, who has been told I will wait until she is eighteen, or until her father allows her to speak with me.

In this whole sequence of events there have also been two Arab male individuals, who interfere into my business and even molest a daughter of mine, along with the young blonde, who they attempt to persuade away from me. It is now Christmas Eve and they are all standing around the streets terrorizing each other, but no one will come to say hello and break the monotony, as I wait homeless. This poem is therefore titled "I'll Knock for You."

Long Recipe

The ingredients have come from many different places.
The list is a very long one in which there are those that are hard to find.
Bat wings, frog legs, caterpillars, and maybe even shoes with laces.
Without a doubt the ingredients are of a different kind.

The list gets even longer, as time goes by.
To foreign places and beyond I must travel, before my recipe is filled.
The aroma is so sweet and I even have to cry.
The pot simmers away and I'm sure I will be thrilled.

With zeros and ones, maybe with those of a nun.
The fragrance fills the air and it looks like gold.
A most enjoyable meal when it is done.
The table setting will have silver and platinum, the napkins
a special fold.

Rhinoceros horns, a monkey's brain, maybe parts of a train.
I keep stirring and stirring, but it will never be cold.
A long recipe and the ingredients are even brought by a crane.
It's a long recipe and the ingredients will never be sold.

With a large wooden spoon I stir, and soon.
At the end of the list shall come one with a typhoon.
One who travels with a raccoon.
A long recipe and I'll taste it like a loon.

12-24-07   Mr. Bad

This poem is titled "Long Recipe" because of the fact that I have been working on a way to win back my losses, after my divorce from an eighteen year marriage. At the time of my divorce my wife was granted the children, the house, and most of the cash that was available. I traveled once again to the United States divorced and looking for a new life. I have now written several poetry books, drawn plans for a patent, which has an agreement to proceed, have plans to publish all my poetry on some twenty compact disc, and I have created two music compact disc, which are prepared for recording and have entered over seventy-two thousand sweepstakes and lotteries world wide. I also have been working towards three degrees and a new wife, who has been following me for some time now and spends all her time in the outdoors.

Tweak from a Twine!

Like the pink panther I search for a clue.
In corners, cracks, and crevices I wonder what is true.
Beneath rocks, in bushes, behind trees, and even up in the blue.
There must be something that will lead me to you.

With binoculars I view the pastures, valleys, hills, and the great divide.
I search and search, but it can't be denied.
With a magnifying glass I glance, as I try to decide.
I sense there is something missing and that I have been deprived.

Finger prints, foot tracks, smeared dust, scuff marks,
something must be to find.
With stethoscope and tweezers, I'll find some kind.
I look and look, am I so blind?
Through oceans and forest I travel and I'm still behind.

A thump, a bump, my throat received a lump.
A scratch, a scream, maybe I'll find a clump.
A bang, a clang, is there someone with a rump?
A ding, a wong, perhaps behind the stump.

Somewhere is something and I know she is so fine.
I search and search, so that I may dine.
There, what is it, a piece of pine?
I tweak from a twine!

12-25-07   Mr. Bad

This is a poem that expresses how I look for clues that will lead me to the truth that there really is a young blonde following me around. I have never met her, as of yet in my life, but have become to have a tremendous amount of love for her. Her voice, along with others' who are following me talk about me and their voices are clear. The story, which is behind this poem is that I have chased through fields, driven around on a bicycle, and even ran through and around street overpasses looking to catch this young blonde, who follows me, but was never able to see or catch her. This poem is titled "Tweak from a Twine!" to also express that I have become so very much in love with this young blonde, who I have never met and have only viewed her picture on the local radio station's web-site for which she was employed. The point is that from just her voice or a minute twine I have been thrown deeply in love with her and yearn, or tweak for her.

The Final Scripts

From the beginning to the end I thought they would have come
to mend.
From the first letter to the last it ends with such a vast cast.
The words are like an omen, but they will defend.
I have received the help from God, as he has shown thou hast.

Time has laid a path of catacombs to ancient places.
The free and the Cree shall be known of those that have fought
to have been seen.
Like an adventure from pyramids on the Nile to the deepest jungles
with faces.
Through the renaissance of the unknown or to a future
that shall have been.

Dark ages and the strongest cages could not withhold all the rages.
The deepest waters and the steepest mountains are ways,
which must be taken.
Doctrines and those in moccasins tell tales of all these pages.
A deed shall become of need and be God forsaken.

Like sand through an hour-glass we fulfill our lives and as waters do we
also change our tides.
As does a flower absorb the rain so do we all prosper each day with God.
It is he, who has the belief and faith that abides.
A journey of a thousand places in which there is the weird and even the odd.

11-27-07   Mr. Bad

"The Final Scripts" is a poem written to say that, through all that I have been, which has been written in Poetic Shades of Life 1, 2, 3 and this book, The Final Scripts, along with Poetry of the Times and a German book titled, Geschichte aus einem Leben (story from a life), I will succeed and proceed on with my life. All the mental stress and terror, the depression, the lies, and all the games that have been played upon me will not deprive me of a great future. The poetry in this book and the others is to me like the works of God's own. I have been forced through some really harsh times and the deceiving, which has been around me will not succeed over me. The poetry I have written shall be truth for people to read, as to who has been correct and incorrect, as I have gone through a very depressing time poor and homeless against what has been done to me. I can only hope that the poetry has been enjoyed and many people from the ancient living to new times would get the opportunity to enjoy it.

Thank You

The End